My Lonely Love

WRITTEN BY:
JOHNA BOTTORFF

COVERT ART BY:
CASEY SHEEDY

INTRODUCTION

This is by far the toughest thing I've ever done. Putting my thoughts down on a page and then sharing them with people I know and don't know. It honestly makes me feel sick to my stomach, but as ironic as it sounds it is my dream to publish a book all on my own. If you are reading this page, that means my book looked interesting enough for you to pick up. Thank you, even if you don't buy this book (i hope you do), I just want to say thank you for at least picking it up.

I know people say "I started this during the pandemic..." Well that is true for this. As a semi practicing catholic (Dad and Grandma forgive me) i needed to do something during Lent.

Instead of giving up something like I always do, I decided to start something. I put a literal pen to paper and wrote. All I had during the pandemic was time to think about this crazy love story I had in my head. One that absolutely decimated me. Even now as I think back it still hurts me, everything that went on, and everything that was said. After a while slowly but surely I started to pull myself back together, but not as the person I was before. I'm still broken, but who isn't?

When you read this group of poems, I hope that it makes you feel a little less alone, and a little less lonely, because sometimes loving someone can be the loneliest thing in the world. Thank you for spending your well earned money and your very precious time reading all the thoughts that have swam in my head for years.

If no one tells you today, you are loved, you matter, drink water, and remember to take care of yourself. There are people who do love you, and will love you no matter what. And that includes me.

DEDICATION

This book is dedicated to all the people who have had to find themselves again after heartbreak.

I'm so proud of you, keep going!

"This is a love story to all my old memories..."
-Hoodie Allen

"Wonder if you are still thinking about me, cause I just wrote all these songs about you..."
-Hoodie Allen

(Yes, I put in two quotes by Hoodie. If you know me don't act surprised!)

I hope that when you read this you are not upset.

I hope that you see this as a sign of healing and not hatred.

I hope that when you read this that you see just how much you meant to me.

I hope that when you read this, you see just how much love is still there.

I hope that when you read this, you see just how much I still absolutely care about you.

I hope that when you read this that you'll call.

I absolutely hope that when you read this you remember the good times like I do.

I pray that when you read this you keep an open mind.

I pray that when you read this, that you will continue to hold me in your heart.

I hope that when this is over, I feel better and that I can move on.

I hope that when you read this, you'll have a look as to what goes on in this anxious mess i call my mind.

I remember the day I met you.

I was shy and nervous, you were loud and funny.

You said whatever came to mind, and you encouraged me to do so.

I started to feel my shoulders loosen, and the butterflies to subside.

Little did I know that that first day would be the start of my downfall.

What are the things I love about you?

Your laugh

Your smile

The look in your eyes when you're happy

The way that you smell.

There are a million more things to love.

It's you, and I wish it wasn't.

You are not for me and I am not for you.

Yet, here I am madly in love with you.

Tomorrow is it.

You'll finally be in my space.

I'm nervous and scared,

But if i'm honest i'm excited.

Sometimes when I see you my heart does not flutter.

Sometimes when I hear your voice my knees do not go weak.

Sometimes I do not miss you or the way that you always smiled at me.

But that is only sometimes...

I waited for you to see me waiting for you.

I'd hoped you were waiting for me too.

You, however, are waiting for someone else.

I wait for the day to come when you don't dance around my brain,

Like a tap dancer who won't sit down.

I waited,

And waited,

And waited for you.

But you took your sweet time,

Every minute that I waited,

My heart leapt at the thought of you.

I watched the door for hours,

But you never walked in.

I thought of you today,

And I smiled.

I thought of our jokes and our laughs.

The looks of knowing but never achieving.

All we have is our looks forever, we were not meant to be.

The day that i fell was a day for the books.

Nothing spectacular, just a normal day.

We sat and we talked a little longer than normal

When I turned to look in your eyes, something made my breath hitch.

My stomach dropped, and I kind of wanted to vomit.

It was a feeling I hadn't felt before.

I wrote it off as nothing, maybe just a cramp.

But it happened again the next day, and the day after.

I told my best friends, and we all agreed that it was love.

That day, it changed everything.

It changed me forever.

I'm exhausted from being in love with you.

Do I really love you?

Why should i?

Do you even care about me?

I have to stop waiting for you,

You've never waited for me.

If i could live the same day over and over,

I would like to meet you every single day.

That way I could remember that feeling I had when I first met you.

That way you could never break my heart like I knew you would.

15

The first time you left me,

I was devastated by the loss of you.

I had never felt so betrayed in all my young life.

The person i seemed to be looking for my whole life,

They left me without a second thought.

I remember when you called to explain.

All the anger left my heart when you said hello.

Lame as it sounds, I forgave you that exact second.

My heart would've rather forgiven you than to be angry with you.

If that doesn't tell you how much I loved you then,

All you needed to do was just say hello.

If only i had been a little bit older,

Or maybe if you had been a little bit younger.

If only we had met before the world decided our fate.

What if the deck was not stacked against us?

Would we have had a chance?

But that wasn't the hand we were dealt.

Fate had already decided she needed to intervene.

Do you remember that day in the car?

When you drove me home, and all I could say was thank you when it was over?

It was all i could wish that you wouldn't ask to come in,

That you wouldn't need to use the bathroom, or even want a glass of water.

I was terrified in the car thinking of all the scenarios that would never happen.

I could have thrown up on that ride home.

You always wanted to know more, but I never wanted you to know more.

The more you knew about me, the more you would see that I was no one special.

I wanted to be special to you, to a certain extent.

You loved me like a kid and I loved you more than that.

I wish I would have been brave enough to just enjoy the ride knowing it was the one and only time.

I would have talked and laughed and sang along to songs with you.

But instead I was paralyzed with fear, you were never supposed to know what I felt inside.

I was going to take it to my grave, but now we both get to do that.

And it doesn't make me feel the least bit better.

What I wouldn't give to ride in the car with you one more time.

I wish that you could have read my mind all those months ago.

Then you could have told me not so subtly that it would never work.

I knew it couldn't.

But if you'd read my mind you could have answered all my questions, and you could have eased my racing thoughts.

If we could read each other's minds, maybe we could be around each other.

Maybe we could be better but never the same.

Maybe then, when I'm thinking about you, you could tell me to stop.

Maybe when I think I see more, you could tell me there was nothing more.

Maybe if you could read my mind my thoughts would never have jumped to so many conclusions.

It would save me the shame and embarrassment.

Maybe if you could have read my mind we would be speaking, instead of sitting in this drowning ocean of silence.

If only we could read each other's minds.

Days with you are (sort of) easy,

Nights without you are hard.

What i wouldn't give to have my head on your chest,

Listening to your heart beat.

Days without you are tough,

I sit and I wonder ""what are you doing?"

"Are you thinking about me, like I'm thinking about you?"

I know that you aren't,

But I cannot help but wonder, what if you are?

I need a good and restful sleep,

Where my dreams are sweet and true.

But when I wake up happy, it's because I get to see you.

With sun shining in your eyes, and your hair all tousled.

That's all I've ever dreamed of.

Last night I kissed you for the first time.

We'd been dancing and we tripped over our feet.

You were right on top of me looking at me like you'd just realized I was it for you.

Then you leaned down and kissed me soft, then more fervently.

You tasted like a pack of sweet tarts.

I felt your whole weight on top of me and I just wanted to lay there and feel your lips forever.

But we had to get up before someone saw us.

That kiss was not supposed to be.

Then we both knew something that no one else knew and could never find out.

I smiled to myself knowing that even for just a few seconds I was able to call you mine.

Then my eyes started to flutter and then I was in my bed in the real world.

You weren't there next to me, and that kiss lingered on my lips and started to fade.

Then it was all gone and I remembered I've never kissed you before.

I dreamt of you last night,

For the first time in a long time.

You were next to me, scratching my scalp like you'd done it a million times.

The second time, you laid right next to me in the bed.

You wrapped your arms around me,

You stayed until I fell asleep.

When I woke up you weren't actually there, and that broke me the hardest.

Not a lot to say today,

But I missed you and thought of you all day.

But how is that different from any other day?

I hope I can find the words to tell you everything.

If I have to leave you, I will.

It'll hurt like hell,

But I'll do it for both our sakes.

She told me that she loved you,

And I cried all the way home.

It seemed like you loved her too,

The calls, texts, and voicemails,

It was everything I wanted.

But you only wanted to give that to her,

Because you absolutely would never give that to me.

I wanted the hours of phone time, and the long thread of texts.

But all I got was left on read, and half hearted apologies.

The worst part of it?

I still wanted what you had with her, a reciprocated relationship.

Life never does the things we want it to.

Oh the fights that we had.

The knock down drag outs, that left us both feeling like we should be better.

The words that we always thought that finally came out, just to hurt the other person.

I remember every one, and every damn word that broke my heart in the process.

But it was the calls and texts after.

I could hear the regret in your tone.

You said you were sorry, and being the hopeless person I am, I forgave you every time.

The ball is in your court,

That's where it's going to be forever.

I think i'm okay with that,

You can keep the ball.

I don't think I want it anymore.

I told you everyday,

Even on the days I never saw you.

When i said those words for real,

I knew you would not feel them too.

I thought you needed to know,

I had to say it or I would combust.

You said those words back to me,

What you said were the same words,

But they meant something different.

When I saw you today it was like the first time.

When i looked at you and knew,

I would be a wreck after you were through with me.

Here we are doing this dance and I have to pretend that everything is okay.

When you weren't there I thought it was gone.

I thought all the remnants of you had disappeared forever.

Now you're back and so are the feelings.

The pains in my chest when I see you.

I'm trying not to laugh too hard at your jokes.

I'm trying not to stare for too long.

It was like this before it ruined everything for me.

You're not mine to love, but God do I love you.

Looking back i thought it best

To put you somewhere far from the rest.

I put you in my heart for safe keeping.

But you punched, kicked, and stabbed,

Trying to claw your way out.

You ripped right through me,

I tried to put my heart back together again.

But the broken pieces never fit together the same.

Rain or shine,

Day in and day out.

When I am sitting at my desk,

When I am lying in my bed.

I am always wondering when I will see you again.

You left me, and you didn't say goodbye.

I thought you cared for me,

But that was clearly a lie.

Maybe i'm being stupid,

Or maybe I misread the signs.

All i know is that i miss you,

Everyday, rain or shine.

We're different now.

The looks are not same,

And the talking is different.

Pretty sure i ruined everything

You know how I feel, but how do you feel?

Is there something you are not telling me?

I just want some honesty,

Please tell me how you feel.

I knew you wouldn't be there.

I expected it.

It doesn't hurt me any less,

I just wish for once you would keep your word.

You'll never be able to let me go...

Do you remember saying that to me?

Little did you know how right you were.

I thought you meant it when you said it.

I thought nothing would ever come between us.

But I was wrong, there was one thing.

And that changed everything between us.

It's hard when we don't talk.

When we are together though,

It's like nothing changed.

It's different now,

I know we are not meant to be.

Why do I even try?

What about you makes me want to lose it all?

I hope i can draw a line in the sand,

And I hope I'm strong enough not to cross it.

I don't want you to love me,

I just want you to be with me like we've always been.

I want you to be my friend, that's all.

I don't know why you don't get that.

I've probably lost you forever,

That does not make me love you less.

Eventually, I will love you, but not the way I do now.

I'll love you like I love everyone else.

Just friends and never anything more.

Not ever again.

There have been many laughs, tears,

And more heartfelt talks than you could imagine.

Somethings have to end,

It seems like you picked the day.

I was just there waiting.

I went by your cue and now,

We've taken our bows,

Time to say goodbye.

I didn't regret telling,

Not until you made me feel like it didn't matter.

Like somehow I put a burden on you.

I'm sorry i bothered you,

I won't do it again.

I didn't miss you as much today.

I was scared that you would show and then you didn't.

A weight lifted off me when I didn't see you.

I have not heard your voice in days,

There has been only silence.

It is not as bad as I thought it would be.

Somehow, it's comforting.

43

If you would have asked I would have ran with you.

I would have hopped in whatever car or on whatever motorcycle and rode off into the sunset.

I would have grabbed a bag and went wherever you went.

I would have held you when it all became too much.

I would have put my head on your chest when I wanted to be close to you.

I would have blocked out the world with you and traveled all over.

It's hard to think that I would have dropped it all for you.

But you couldn't even pick me.

I have not heard from you,

I doubt you will say anything.

That is the one thing I have accepted.

It has to be over now.

45

I'm such a sap.

All I could think about was hearing your voice.

When I heard it, I almost burst into tears.

I didn't think I would still miss you this much.

It's been over a year and here I am still missing you.

And you're clearly not missing me.

No calls, no text backs, and me not on your mind.

Maybe you're better off without me,

Somewhere inside me I know I'm better without you.

But I would rather be bad with you, then great without you.

Like I said I'm a sap for you.

Too bad that's where you got off the train.

I just gave you another reason to let me go.

And you let go of that rope like it was on fire.

Too bad I was still holding on,

Just hoping you wouldn't let me go.

Many things have changed over this time.

I told you I loved you without any expectation.

You shut me out and left me wondering,

What had I done wrong?

You left me for too long.

Then i realized,

I did not want you to love me,

I wanted to move on from it.

You clearly were stuck in it, paralyzed.

But me?

I was free.

The love I had for you is forever.

You are burned onto my heart,

I will say goodbye for now.

Until the day when we can speak again,

Like we always did before.

When i've come to my senses,

I won't think about you all day.

My heart won't ache when we're apart

I will not cry myself to sleep thinking of what can never be,

Today i felt all those things,

More love for you than for me.

With all the sadness and tears,

Loving you is my biggest fear.

Talking to you used to be easy,

It used to be fun. Now all I feel is my heart coming undone.

I thought i could stop the feelings from coming back,

I thought there would be no more pain.

I fell for you,

Now all I do is wait for it to rain.

Waiting for lightning to strike,

Hopefully it stops my heart.

That it will finally make it stop.

I hate when people say "you can't help who you love."

Because I hated myself for loving you.

The absolute shame I felt when I realized I'd fallen for you.

The things I said to myself for being such a crazy young woman in love.

How could you possibly love this man? Don't you know that he can't and won't ever be yours?

Don't you know that he will absolutely laugh in your face?

Don't you know he will give you the same look as all the others?

That "i don't want to hurt your feelings, i think that we should absolutely stand friends" look.

That "I can't and won't ever see you that way, but we can totally try to make this work but it won't because now i'm weirded out by this."

I wish that I could have fallen for someone else.

But like they say I couldn't help it.

You found your way into my heart,

And I'm still paying for it, even after you are gone.

I fell for the guy who wasn't mine,

I thought maybe he would fall for me too.

But the joke was on me,

He would never fall for me.

I wish i could stop falling,

Falling for people who don't love me.

For people who are out of my reach,

For people who love other people.

For people who can't see me.

I wish to stop falling for people who will never love me back.

In a perfect world perhaps,

A dream of a naive girl possibly.

I want to stop falling,

My heart can't take too much more.

Why can I only love someone who loves someone else?

Why can I only imagine them realizing that it's actually me that they want?

Why am I so fucked up in the head? Why do I always want what I can never have?

Was it that I felt like I was always vying for someone's love as a child?

Was I never told that I was loved enough?

Is it just the convenience of the fact that I know we could never be?

Maybe it's the fact that I get all the benefits of a relationship without actually having to stress about it.

At least that's what some therapist told me.

I can't remember a time when I didn't want what wasn't mine.

That's why my heart can never heal, I always want what I can't have.

I want love with someone who loves someone else?

That makes no sense, if only I could rearrange this brain. Keep it from telling my heart all the wrong things.

And my heart would have listened to all the things that were wrong, and I wouldn't have fallen.

Then I wouldn't be sitting here in the dark writing about someone who was never meant for me.

I wish I knew why I was like this, and how I could make it stop.

I'm tired of trying, tired of chasing,

And for once I want someone to want me.

Want me like I've wanted everyone.

To love me for life, not just for a second.

54

I'll always love you more,

And that is okay.

I'll always look at you with adoration in my eyes.

I'll always want to be near or around you no matter what.

I'll always want more,

But I know I can't have it.

Your love didn't kill me,

My love for you killed me.

I walked past someone who looked remarkably like you.

I lost my breath just looking at him,

I swore it was you.

I walked a little faster, and my breathing got shallower.

I realized that i'm not ready,

Fuck, i dont think i'll ever be ready.

After all this time I thought that if I saw you I would feel differently.

But I was fooling myself, I only saw someone who looked like you and it almost brought me to tears.

Maybe it's okay that I'll never see you again.

Maybe it's okay that I'm not ready.

My worst fear in life is seeing you, and having to make small talk like nothing ever happened.

It makes me cry just thinking about it.

I've made a playlist that makes me think of you.

I'm just not as ready as I thought I was.

Maybe, I'm not as strong as I thought I was.

When I'm up at 3 am and the world is dark and quiet.

I looked through all our old messages, ones I totally forgot were even there.

My eyes tear up because who could have guessed this is where we'd be.

When I'm up at 3 am I remember all the 3 am texts we sent just cause we knew we were up.

Remember when we would spend hours together and talk until the sun was high in the sky?

We would go out separate ways, and I couldn't wait until 3 am the next day.

3 am is my least favorite time of day, it just reminds me that even though I know you're not sleeping, I can't reach out.

I can't see what you're thinking about, and you can't know what's on my mind.

3 am is my least favorite time of day. It's the time that was once safe for us to be us.

Now it's just a dark time of day, when I roll over to turn my tv on, so the noise of something can put me into a dreamless sleep.

3 am is my least favorite time of day because that's the time of day when I miss you the most, and it's okay to cry about it.

Because no one is listening, and there's no one around to judge me.

3 am is the worst time of day, I wish that one day I could sleep past it, so there would be no pain.

But only lovely, restful sleep.

Yesterday I was praising space.

Today i closed the space between us,

My heart got heavy, with the weight I thought I'd lost.

I wish I didn't love you so much, and that I could lose that weight forever.

But it seems that my heart will be overweight for you, until it stops beating.

I remember when the sound of your voice would make my heart flutter.

Now the sound makes my heart drop.

It's the soundtrack to my nightmares.

The ones where you see and you speak but it's cold.

The worst sound that happens in these nightmares is when you're silent.

When you see me and you don't speak, and then you walk away as if you never knew me.

Then the sound of my sobs and the cracking of my heart because the pain is so intense.

The worst part of the nightmares is waking up and realizing that all of my nightmares have come true.

You came to me in a dream,

You got into my car while the sky cried.

You said the words that i've wanted for so long,

"I'm sorry," you said.

For all the cruel words you'd said,

For all the months we went without speaking.

"I'm sorry that this happened,"

You hugged me and even though the sky cried,

All around us, I felt sadness.

I knew that this was the end,

This was the last time we'd speak.

I opened my eyes to a sad mind and a broken heart.

Too bad it was only a dream, and I'll never get those words from the real you.

Maybe you're not sorry, or maybe you don't know how to say it.

I just want two words to (hopefully) move on.

My dreams are telling me that I need to move on.

That I need to let go of you.

For the sake of my mind and my heart.

To find someone who will love me and not tear me apart.

It will be hard, we had so many laughs together.

But now it's time for me to let you be,

I finally get to be free.

I'll still look back on our time together and smile.

I might even shed a tear for the lost friendship.

But I'll be happier without you, and you'll be better without me.

I'll miss you today and a little less every day.

Nothing about losing us makes me happy.

But I know that it's best to let go.

One day I'll see you out and it won't break my heart and we'll laugh about the good times.

You were the only person that I ever really loved.

But it's no one's fault, and we can try as hard as we can.

But we know we can't control our feelings.

I still love you as I did before.

But it'll grow less and less, and finally I won't be such a mess.

Maybe I am ready to let you go, but not without tears.

I'll love you everyday forever, but I have to let you go.

It's amazing to me that I still miss you.

I still want to feel your arms wrapped around me,

Holding me tightly, making me feel like I matter more than anything.

We've been silent for months now, at least to each other.

We've talked to the same people and gotten the same advice.

I've been told i need to let you go,

And the lord knows I'm trying.

It just felt like we would get past this like we always did.

I was wrong,

We can't and we won't.

You'll just turn into a memory in my mind,

You'll make me smile, and you'll make me cry.

You'll still be there, and that's okay.

We need to be apart,

Even though it breaks my fucking heart.

Everything is fine during the day. The sun is shining and I have all the distractions in the world.

But it's at night when I feel hopeless.

When the tv is on to drown out the thoughts, and the sheets are warm from lying in them for hours.

When even my fluffiest pillows, and my softest teddy bears can't stop my heart from racing.

They can't stop my mind from running through everything that happens.

It's the hours it takes to fall asleep, only to wake up four or five times a night.

Not even my dreams have brought me comfort.

When I wake from them I feel the hole in my chest and the anxiety creeping in.

The constant hunger I feel, only to be full in two bites. Then to be starving again two hours later.

It's the time in the shower that I spend crying or at least trying to.

It's picking out the comfiest outfit that's also work appropriate.

It's the driving and listening to sad songs just trying to get the tears that have evaded me for so long.

It's the constant not so constant talking about it that makes it the suck.

It's not wanting to bother anyone with my problems because I know everyone else has more important things going on.

It's just wanting it to be over so I can finally have some Goddamn peace.

But alas that is not my life nor has it been for years.

I pray every night that the lord brings me a peaceful night's sleep and dreams that don't make me want to cry when I wake up.

I just want some peace of mind, that's all I've ever wanted.

I just want the sadness to go away and the pain to finally stop.

But I can't do any of that until I learn to let go of what truly breaks my fucking heart.

It might seem like I didn't fight for my relationship.

Because in hindsight I let my emotions get the better of me.

And they still are to be honest, I can't sleep without replaying that scene over in my head at least 100 times.

I could have said so many things that would have convinced him that we were made for each other.

I could have told him I loved him, somehow hoping he would see it the way I did.

Realize he loved me back, and then vow that we would make it work.

But what is the point in telling someone how you feel when you know it won't save anything.

You'll still stop talking, you'll still stop texting, and you'll look at your pictures together and wish to go back to how it used to be.

But, you can change the past and as much as it fucking hurts, you have to try and move on.

There are tears involved, a lot of them.

Once the sobs subside and you fall into a dreamless sleep in your bed.

For a few hours everything is just okay.

Then you wake up and do it over and over again, until one day they stop.

One day it doesn't hurt so bad, one day you'll smile at the thought of them.

But that day is not today, and it won't be any day soon.

I remember the nights I couldn't sleep. The dreams that would bring me to tears when I woke up.

They don't tell you that life isn't like the movies.

Just because you love someone doesn't mean it'll be reciprocated.

Just because you want them all to yourself doesn't mean you get them.

They don't tell you that you'll sit and cry for days and days.

That there is no happy upbeat campy music that signifies that everything is going to be okay.

There's only scouring the internet for sad songs you've never heard because you know that they'll understand you more than a person.

They don't tell you that you'll cry yourself to sleep, and that your stomach drops at just the thought of them.

That your breath is going to catch when you see a picture of them after not seeing them for a while.

That you're going to have shitty sleep because you don't know why they won't talk to you.

You just want to scream at them but you can't. Screaming isn't what you do.

You keep it in until you ultimately explode.

Most days I'm fine. Nothing insane to report, wake up, go to work, come home, watch tv and eat and then go to bed.

But sometimes while I'm driving down the interstate I think of you.

I think about whether you're driving safely to your destination.

If you are drinking enough water and getting enough sleep.

Then for a slight moment I think about whether you think about me.

If you bring me up in conversation like I do you.

If you worry about my mental health as much I do yours.

Wonder if you feel just as bad about how things went down between us.

Wondering if you regret anything you said to me, and if all you want to do is call and apologize.

Hoping you pull up my contact in your phone, and hover over the message button.

Pulling up our old text threads to see if we could have handled things differently.

But wishing so desperately that you could see me in person to talk things out face to face.

Do you bring me up to our mutual friends? Do they tell you how I'm doing?

How am I trying to forget about you? And how I sometimes wish I hadn't gotten attached.

I just worry and wonder about you every so often.

Then I hope that you are happy because you were so unhappy when we left it.

I hope you never take that happiness for granted.

And I hope with all my heart that you hope that I am happy too.

Someday I will be happy, even if it is without you.

Have you ever had an anniversary?

But not to celebrate something happy,

A day where you remember something fucked up.

Something that is only significant to you, but you can't tell anyone for fear of being judged.

I've only ever had one, and it's a day that has stuck in my head for months.

The date when I told you I loved you.

The date when I decided that enough was enough and I would just tell you.

I would squash that feeling once and for all.

That day is today, the 7th day of the 2nd month.

A day that lives in my head rent free because it's the day we changed.

The day you stopped being my friend,

But you pretended you would be.

The day where you swore nothing would ever change us, not even unrequited love.

This day changed everything, and how sometimes I wish I would've stopped myself. If I'd only have waited.

Waited until we would possibly never see each other again.

Wait until I see you again and see if I still feel the same way.

Even though I haven't seen you, even though this day lives in me and only me.

I still love you, and today is a day I want to cry and scream and call you and tell you I'm sorry that I fucked us up.

But I can't, I know you wouldn't answer the phone.

Happy anniversary, for many more tearful filled years to come.

It's been almost a year since we spoke,

A year since i saw the pain in your eyes,

A year since we both said things we (hopefully) didn't mean.

I've tried not to miss you,

I've tried not to call or text.

But I'm a sucker for you.

I've seen you in my dreams and my nightmares.

I've cried because I can't believe it.

You left me out on the curb like a garbage can,

But I still have you on a pedestal.

I wish i could say i missed you for different reasons,

Good reasons, that made sense to me and other people.

I can't tell anyone how much i miss you,

Or how many calls I've almost dialed, and how many times I've almost

texted you.

For you,

You get to thrive, and live the life you always thought you would have.

For me?

I got sad songs, and then cried myself to sleep.

Or the nights where the anxiety of it all keeps me up until the sunrises.

I can't say that I never think of you, or even that I don't miss you.

That simply is not true.

I wish it wasn't but here i am,

I'm writing poetry about you because I can't do anything else.

There was a time when I could tell you whatever came to mind.

But this time I have to keep it to myself.

God, when will this end?

You can't say I never tried.

I always wanted to talk, I always wanted to clear the air.

You didn't,

One call, a few texts, but never any follow through.

I learned long ago that there is no such thing as closure.

I would sit and wait forever, but damn I just don't have the time.

When I talked to you the other day, I almost vomited.

Not because I didn't want to and not because I was nervous.

I just was not expecting to hear your voice in my ears.

We talked and talked like nothing bad ever happened between us.

We laughed and joked and caught up on life.

It's been three years and talking to you felt like no time had passed at all.

God, did i fucking miss you so much.

I felt the weight lift off my shoulders,

And I cried for the thousandth time.

But it was a happy cry,

It was the cry I'd been holding in.

I realize how badly i just wanted to talk to you,

I wanted our normal back.

I finally got my friend back, I finally found the normal rhythm of my heart.

I finally can stop looking behind me.

I listened to that song for the first time, and let me tell you it was not by choice.

I was standing in a crowd full of people, I heard the opening bars, and my heart stopped beating.

There was nowhere for me to go, I was stuck in a sea of people who didn't know what that song was doing to me.

You wouldn't remember, but you played it for me one day.

A song I would have never guessed that you loved.

I even made it your ringtone.

Just because when you called it would make me smile.

Here I was paralyzed by the song, and I had no way out.

I still can't hear that song without wanting to cry for what once was.

I can just avoid the song forever.

But we know that's impossible.

Writing out my feelings for someone who does not give me a second thought.

When this is over I might still be sad, i might cry, and i may even miss you.

But it is better to let it go and remember what it was.

It'll only ever be in the past,

I need to look ahead.

Because someone out there will give me everything one day.

Even after tomorrow,

I will love you still.

I'll think about you,

I'll want to talk to you,

And hug you tighter than ever.

That is not us anymore,

We have to be okay with that.

I know you will never love me too.

That is fine is with me,

I'll love myself more from now on.

I talk about you constantly,

More than I should.

You've consumed all my senses for years,

I am bursting at the seams.

Once i let you go,

My strength will come back.

I've taken time and thought. And tried to solve a puzzle that seemed like it was unsolvable.

I thought you were the missing piece but it turns out that you were never going to fit.

You were too big for the space I tried to put you in.

You would never shrink down to fit, not even for me.

Then that pedestal I had you on started to crumble.

The stone started to fall and shower me with cuts and bruises.

Then you were in front of me, a little taller but not up so high.

I finally got to see your face, and everything I remember loving about it.

But I saw you for what you were, a person who would never look at me with the admiration I had for you.

Sometimes I think, was it actually love I felt? Or was it intense admiration?

Whatever it was it crippled me into this fear of losing you in my life.

I didn't want you to leave me because you were the only person that I thought could keep me together.

I never wanted to let you go.

But I had to because once you came down from that pedestal and looked at me.

All I saw was someone who didn't and couldn't truly be any more to me.

Once it all crumbled and came crashing down, I felt the tear dam burst and I was finally free.

Of course some days I miss you and want to reach out.

But then I have to think about all the months that you never said a word.

You didn't even try.

So I think finally I'm ready to say one final goodbye.

I finally stopped listening. I used to listen around me just to hopefully hear your voice in the crowd.

I looked for you in every tall handsome stranger, with brown eyes.

I try not to sit and think about you, but those numbers are getting smaller.

Now I only talk about the good times we had, about the times I laughed more than the times I cried.

It's been so long I've almost forgotten how broken my heart was.

I get a twinge of hurt every now and then. But it's a hurt that is in the process of healing.

A pain that gets smaller and smaller every day. You didn't make me love you, I fell all on my own.

I felt something that you didn't, and that is okay. I can love you less, and I do.

I won't ever stop loving you and having love for you.

But I can love you less, and that, for me, is enough.

It is amazing what space gives you,

Time to think.

Think about things differently.

About all the little things you would ever do for someone.

Then you think about things that make you happy.

Then you realize all you needed was space and time,

Just to clear the corners of your mind.

I was in the dark searching,

Searching for someone to lead me to the light.

I thought you were the one to lead me there.

Then I found the one that I thought could lead me there,

That someone is me.

I want you to be happy, and I hope you have someone who loves you.

Someone who loves the sound of your heart beating.

Someone who loves the sound of your laugh and listens to every word that you say.

They take your feelings into consideration and they always tell you how they feel.

They always tell you that they love you when you feel unlovable.

I want them to cherish every hug that you give them.

I want them to always be there for you when you feel like your world is crashing down.

I want you to never feel alone and to always feel like you matter to someone.

I hope that you have someone who does all those things for you.

Even if that person can't ever be me.

I wish I could say that you were the one that got away.

I wish I could say that you were the love of my life.

I don't wish that i never loved you,

And I don't wish that I had never met you.

But i do wish i could say thank you

You taught me more about myself.

You taught me that I deserve to love and to be loved unconditionally.

So with all the love in my heart, I just want to say,

Thank you.

Girl meets boy,

Girl falls for the boy.

Girl gets her heart broken by a boy.

Girl cries at night,

Then one day the girl stops.

Girl learns to love herself more than anything and anyone.

Girl lives happily ever after.

The End.

(Read in the past tense)

I hope that when you read this you were not upset.

I hope that you saw this as a sign of healing and not hatred.

I hope that when you read this that you saw just how much you meant to me.

I hope that when you read this, you saw just how much love is still there.

I hope that when you read this, you saw just how much I still absolutely care about you.

I hope that when you read this that you'll call.

I absolutely hope that when you read this, you'll remember the good times like I do.

I pray that when you read this you keep an open mind.

I pray that when you read this, that you will continue to hold me in your heart.

I hope that when this is over, I feel better and that I can move on.

I hope that when you read this, you'll have had a look as to what goes on in this anxiously in love mind.

Hello and goodbye

That is all that we have now.

That is where we started,

And that is where we have to end.

Hello and goodbye

Songs that helped my heart (In no particular order)

1. Eraserface- Hoodie Allen (the whole "BUB" album, really.)

2. Heartbreak Anniversary- GIVEON

3. Bedroom Ceiling- Sody

4. Aftermath- Vaultboy

5. Watching You- Robinson

6. I Don't Wanna Love You Anymore- LANY

7. Hate the Way- G-Eazy (ft. Blackbear)

8. Love Myself- Andy Grammar

9. Crying Over You- The Band Camino

10. Hold On- H.E.R.

11. Before Love Came To Kill Us- Jessie Reyez

12. Lonely- Noah Cyrus

13. Coping- Rosie Darling

14. Internet Stalking- wens

15. Same Room- JP Saxe

16. Reckless- Madison Beer

17. Wish We Never Happened- BLU EYES

18. Rainbow- Kasey Musgraves

19. Someone Who Loved You- Teddy Swims

20. Dawns- Zach Bryan

21. You Didn't- Brett Young

22. I Don't Miss You- JP Saxe

23. Arcade- Duncan Laurence

24. Not Sad Anymore- Clara Mae

25. Missing You- Lauren Weintraub

ACKNOWLEDGMENTS

Man this is like a speech for the Oscars! I've always joked about making an acceptance speech and now it's my time to shine! I would like to thank the Academy... No I'm kidding!

Firstly I would like to thank my parents, my mom, DonnaJo, and my dad, John (may he rest in peace). They always encouraged me to follow my dreams and they didn't bat an eye when I told them I wanted to go to college for creative writing, (who needs a degree for that)? I would like to thank all four of my siblings! AJ, Alex, Alysha, and Danielle, thank you for helping me through something you didn't even know I was going through. Our family spending time together is all I ever need to keep a smile on my face. (Y'all have to let me win Christmas Eve Uno this year, your names are in my book)! Thank you to my best friend Gayle, who was with me through everything. My shoulder to cry on and my sounding board. Thank you to KJ and Patches for being there and supporting me, and putting up with my ridiculousness for the better part of a decade. Thank you to Katie for pushing me to not cut anything from this book, and for always being there when I needed you. Thank you to Ashley from work for helping me workshop this, and being my shoulder to cry on at work. Thank you to Laurren Darr and Left Paw Press for helping get these words off my heart and into the hands of people who will (hopefully) love them. And finally I would like to thank the person who broke my heart. You gave me a reason to grow and become a better version of myself. These words wouldn't exist without you, and for that I am grateful for you.

Thank you for reading this book, I hope it brought every reader exactly what they needed at just the right time. I love you all, and thank you!